Platform
Papers

Quarterly essays from Currency House   No. 1: July 2004

CURRENCY HOUSE

PLATFORM PAPERS
Quarterly essays from Currency House Inc.

Editor*: Dr John Golder, j.golder@unsw.edu.au

Currency House Inc. is a non-profit association and resource centre for the performing arts, with a brief to assert the role of the arts in public and intellectual life by research, informed debate and publication on aesthetic, ethical and economic issues, our culture and scholarship.

Postal address: PO Box 2270 Strawberry Hills, NSW 2012 Australia
Email: info@currencyhouse.org.au
Website: www.currencyhouse.org.au
Business and subscription inquiries: (02) 9314 5389

For our subscription form see back page

Book and cover design by Kate Florance
Typeset in 10.5 Arrus BT
Printed by Hyde Park Press, Adelaide

The publication of *Platform Papers* is assisted by the University of New South Wales.

From the Editor

The essays in this series will not always have an editorial. They will, I hope, need no introduction, but speak clearly and unambiguously for themselves. However, as this essay constitutes the launch of a new project for Currency House, a few words of introduction will not be out of place. Currency House was incorporated in 2001 as a think-tank and resource centre for the performing arts. The initiative of Katharine Brisbane, founding mother of Currency Press, it is an association that exists to stimulate debate on the whole gamut of performing arts and, through lectures and seminars, readings, performances and workshops, aims to demonstrate that the practice of the arts can enrich the fabric of daily life.

Platform Papers is the latest initiative in our publishing program. But do we really need to add another journal to the already overcrowded bookshop shelves? Is there room in the market place for another one? Yes, I believe there is. There is certainly room in the public debate for serious discussion of the arts. Other issues—social, political, industrial, ethical—are abundantly catered for and it is right that they are. But the arts are no less vital to our national well-being;

they are not merely forms of entertainment that exist independently of the 'real world'. They are an imaginative expression of these same issues. But, unlike them, the performing arts do not have a platform of their own. Well, now **Platform Papers** provides one.

These **Platform Papers**, essays commissioned from practitioners and critics across the performing arts, will be a space in which to explore topical ideas, challenge old assumptions, propose new solutions. And to do so at a comfortable length and depth. Historically, the essay as a literary form has generally not thrived in Australia. However, we believe that exponents and supporters of the performing arts, starved of serious discussion in the print media, are hungry for longer think-pieces than a newspaper or monthly magazine can offer.

These papers will not be driven by any single ideological agenda, but aim to reflect a broad spectrum of opinion. And, since we are not about delivering lectures, but stimulating debate, from Paper no. 2 onwards, we shall include a forum section, in which substantial responses to issues raised in the previous essay can be published.

This first essay, by the founding producer of ABC Radio Arts, poet and essayist Martin Harrison, deals with a matter of rising national concern. It is a former insider's considered response to what he, and others, perceive as a moment of crisis. It is feisty and possum-stirring, and a good read. I hope it will provide you with food for thought.

John Golder

'Our ABC' a Dying Culture?

One way forward for arts programming

MARTIN HARRISON

Acknowledgements

Thanks to Barry Hill, Ken Cruickshank, Liz Jacka, Roz Cheney and John Golder, whose different views, even when I have not adopted them, made an invaluable contribution to this essay.

Martin Harrison was founding producer of ABC Radio Art in the 1980s and presented the writers' program *Books and Writing*. He has written extensively for radio and is a widely-published poet. His collection of essays about contemporary poetry and the practice of writing, *Who Wants to Create Australia? and Other Essays* was published this year. He is currently the recipient of an Established Writer's Fellowship from the Australia Council; and teaches writing, sound and radio at the University of Technology, Sydney.

1

The functions of the Corporation are [...] to encourage and promote the musical, dramatic and other performing arts in Australia.[1]

The ABC is not fulfilling its charter obligations in relation to the Australian arts.

There is a long history of budget cuts, poor management appointments, poor policy decisions, Federal Government interference and a lack-lustre Board which lie, in large measure, behind the declining significance of ABC television, radio and online services in the flourishing composition of Australian arts. The ABC has been in trouble in other areas of its activities, too. Its credibility as a news organisation—which, amongst other crucial criteria, means its capacity to remain independent of the views of the government of the day—has been severely challenged.

Its role as an innovative training centre for media professionals, who move on to other broadcasters, has largely disappeared. Its role as a leader and setter of quality standards across Australia's electronic landscape of features, documentary and drama is no longer assured. There is a broad community perception that the current ABC board and management lack compelling policy aims and, under government pressure, have contented themselves with managing the organisation's decline—perhaps even overseeing its partial dismantling before too long.

Nowhere is the problem of decline more strongly felt than in the area of the arts. Arts coverage has gone down markedly. Budgets have been slashed. New programming ideas are thin, and often confused. In the recently created administrative structure, derived from the happily brief, chaotic times of former managing director, Jonathan Shier, there are no substantial administrative positions tasked exclusively with a responsibility to the arts. In TV, the arts and entertainment are folded together. In radio, there are no overarching arts editorial positions. There are few pressures within management which might actively promote the Australian arts as an area of important creative debate or which might creatively enable access to environing art-practices as a major source of program ideas and commissioning in either radio or television. Strikingly, the one recent report on the ABC's arts profile, Liz Jacka's *Arts Programming on ABC Radio, Television and Online* was commissioned, not by management, but 'by the Community and Public Service Union on behalf of its ABC members in ABC

Radio'. [2] It was commissioned, in short, by staff, not because the management or Board wanted to think aloud about the creative future of the organisation, but because of a staff awareness that arts content, commissioning and specialist program-making in the arts are in danger of disappearing.

Given these circumstances, it is an understatement to say that the ABC has been particularly inept at telling viewers and listeners exactly what creative new ideas it has regarding programming, arts programming or otherwise. All too often there is a sense that nobody needs to know, a hope that, if nothing is said and little discussion entered into, then issues such as their failing performance in the arts area will perhaps pass quietly unnoticed. The ABC seems not to have learnt that, whether the issues are large or small, the image problem becomes more rather than less intractable. Whether the question is a very public one—for example, how the sackings, the commercial re-orientation and the staff demoralisation of the Shier period came about—or whether it is a very specialist one—for example, why Classic-FM's only internationally lauded arts program *The Listening Room* was canned—the standard response is to hoist drawbridges and drop portcullises. A stunned, disbelieving audience is left to hear the sound of footsteps racing down the winding stairs into cellars deep within the building.

This bunker mind-set is itself a symptom of the malaise. The ABC is entrusted to be one of our key national centres of critical culture, in other words, one of the places where a national conversation about art, language, cultural aspiration and critical ideas can be carried on in public and participated in by all. This is not what is currently happening. Arts programs on TV are now rare. When they do occur they seem to have been relegated to some other area of quasi-art interest where discussion is down-graded to chat and the art object (the painting, the new film, the new play, the innovative arts documentary) only occasionally in sight. Talk-back abounds on radio, but informed specialist discussion is confined mainly to non-arts programs. Nothing exemplifies the cultural difficulty more readily than the debate about the need for a 'right-wing Phillip Adams' on radio. How will offering a Liberal Party spokesperson serve to open up a wider cultural and critical debate? We do not go to the ABC to get our own views reflected back at us undiluted; only governments do that. That the ABC's responsibility for maintaining a diverse national conversation be reduced to Canberra politics—namely, that critical culture is the same as Labor-versus-Liberal—is not only extraordinarily insulting to ABC audiences, but it suggests that an inner dialogue, an inner policy debate within the ABC is itself intimidated and partisan. Worse, it insults the ABC's long-lived, glorious tradition of liveliness and intellectual independence.

Bunkered down, however, the ABC will find it hard to resist such simplistic, externally imposed paradigms. It cannot be the arena for a nation's open-ended cultural debate when it cannot openly discuss its ideas in relation to the arts, to programming in relation to literature, to creative work in the newer arts and to critical culture generally. Similarly, it is entrusted to be a leading promoter of music and drama—in particular, new work: Section 1(a) of the ABC Act tells it to be 'innovative'—but it cannot fulfil that trust if these are areas which the organisation cannot, or will not, any longer fund. I shall return later to the question of how far the ABC should seek to be more openly involved in a wider set of ideas, discussions and collaboration concerning its arts profile. After all, it is as an activist, an initiator of new ideas, that the ABC has made one of its greatest contributions to the wider cultural life of Australians. There are many ways in which the ABC can, and should, engage proactively with the new and the local.

A further, more immediate, reason for writing this essay, with some of its more uncomfortable and critical passages, is that I sense a broadly-held concern about the direction the ABC has taken in relation to the arts community. And I sense behind that concern further questions about the Corporation's role as a creative broadcaster, some of them deeply troubling. In a way, the ABC's involvement with the Australian arts is of an unusual kind. This involvement covers both talking and reporting on the arts, as much as it does commissioning and producing. Further, the term *art* must here cover work which is defined in traditional format (e.g. a play or a poem) as well as that loosely composed area where media art, television programs and radio works are themselves art objects and art practices. This cross-over between the use of the medium as reportage and the use of the medium as the primary, or at least as a strongly framing, form of artistic representation has, however, been one of the main reasons why writers, playwrights, composers, performers, media artists, critics, innovative filmmakers and comedians etc. have gravitated towards the ABC. The old and the new can be done so well there. The ABC is a space where the best new work, be it on radio, television or online, can be made alongside immediate access to the best of work already made. Or rather, it should be. Currently, there is a deep feeling that the organisation is failing to blend those culturally informative and, at the same time, directly creative aims together.

Most immediately: do enough of us who are practising writers, artists, composers, filmmakers or media artists any longer *expect* the ABC to succeed in an area where currently it so manifestly fails? On the other hand, are *we* any longer a significant part of the ABC's demographic, its target group, whether we are considered consumers *or* makers? Similarly, the view is still widespread that the ABC remains, however inadequately, the key media institution representing the creative interests of writers, artists, filmmakers and playwrights as well as playing a major role in musical culture. But is this so? At this point, questions start to multiply. For if the ABC is not the key national 'thinker' in culture and the arts, why do viewers and listeners agree that it deserves substantial Federal money for a creative and intelligent cultural agenda? Indeed, is the ABC still a serious player in arts and culture? If it is—or wishes to be—what is needed to re-establish ABC media at the heart of current Australian work, whether in the world of letters and writing, in drama, in film, in media art, in digital art practice, in commentary and discussion? After all, isn't this central creative space the one it ought to occupy? Isn't this one of its core roles?

2

Past is past. I salute that various field.[3]

I ncessantly to follow one's own track,' says Montaigne, 'is to be one's own slave.'[4] In the mid-1980s I spent several years producing on contract for ABC Radio National (henceforth RN), presenting *Books and Writing*, producing drama for the ABC Classic-FM *Images* series, and producing feature programs on writers and poets. Later I was one of the moving forces in the formation of what later became the Acoustic Arts Unit, a team of producers who are still alive on the ABC arts scene and who combine a mix of interests in new music, in media and online art, in contemporary writing, in performance work and theatre. Before that I'd freelanced extensively for ABC, mainly script-writing and writing for sound. I remember my first direct encounter with the *milieu*, the world, of the then 2-FC in the late '70s and early '80s: in particular, I recall my sense of what an extraordinary group of playwrights, play producers, literary journalists, and arts and culture feature makers had somehow been assembled there. True, that idyllic image had its war-torn context: some of those producers were refugees from the days when commercial radio produced extensive drama series. Talks, features, music and drama were the four edges of our still largely mono world. There were people charged—yes, actually invited—to take on the task of running poetry programs. There were book programs emanating from both Sydney and Melbourne, drawing in reviewers and writers from around the country. There was a lively editorial process around solicited and unsolicited drama scripts. There was an engagement with critical ideas and with writers, playwrights, poets and novelists who came into the offices and negotiated scripts and reviews and feature items. Actors—new, untried, famous and very famous—came into our studios for bit parts and for long parts. Often, the more famous you were the shorter the sound byte, which was odd until you thought what fees were payable.

There was an ongoing debate and engagement with the new, more experimental music community. There was a sense that ABC Radio played a significant role— I stress, *a* significant role—in helping develop new writers and arts journalists, new playwrights, musical people and novelists. At the same time, it would have been crystal-clear that the ABC and, in particular, what is now RN had, if not a publicly-planned, then government-backed, role in relation to the arts, yet certainly it had adopted an actively persuasive role in representing the best ideas about drama, music and writing to the wider Australian audience. And it was not just talk: the dramas were going to air, as were new poems, innovative features, on-location documentaries, the beginnings of sound works. For many in the intellectual and arts communities, the station was indispensable listening.

Let me continue on this tack for a moment longer. Young though I was, I realised that I had encountered one of those rare moments in any organisation, where the medley of local ideas also engaged cleverly and critically with the best from overseas. There was a confident cosmopolitanism in the air: program makers read and tracked down the best of foreign writers, filmmakers, artists, art-scholars and critics. These were the days when writers' festivals were not largely commercial set-ups, and when overseas travel, overseas books and access to overseas shows and people were, relatively speaking, rarities. If sometimes the response to international work struck me as too eclectic, too hit-and-miss, to add up to more than just informative programming, I had a genuine sense that the people who were making work for the station were testing out the wider contexts of ideas, literature, theatre and media; nor were they just repeating what the publicist, local or international, had on offer. There was money to commission new pieces, to invite writers to write, critics to talk, money to engage performers and composers in experimental work, money to set up interviews overseas—true, not much money, but enough to bring a lively group of freelancers, literary writers, dramatists and actors into the station. These were the floating interest-group, the actors and directors working in theatre or film, or the literary writers writing for the papers, or the writers who were teaching or publishing or editing. Some hung out for work because they depended on it. Others came to check you out and see if they could make a program, pitch a commission, write a review or a talk. They included names which are now amongst the country's best-known. If my personal focus on this media milieu was through literary criticism, poetry and performance, I am sure that something very similar was occurring in the music area too.

I feel no nostalgia for those days. So many factors in the wider media environment have changed since then. To go back there one has to imagine a time which was without online media, had still to develop much of its current access to university and postgraduate education, or in which cosmopolitanism had not been supplanted by the global, multi-ethnic sense of art, ideas and culture which most of us now have. For another thing, when I think back more closely, I seem to have forgotten how there was, as there still is, a constantly politicised public issue to do with the organisation's funding base. Though very differently motivated as appointments, there was even, in the brief tenure of Geoffrey Whitehead as managing director, a pre-quel of the Shier fiasco. In hindsight, too, it's easy to see that, despite the wrangling and earlier cuts under Malcolm Fraser, the mid-'80s were the last time when the ABC had anything approaching an adequate budget. Even so, there was the inevitable internal competition about how to maintain the drama and features' budgets. News and TV wanted everything. There was constant pressure, too, from hostile Federal governments: bad-tempered, one-eyed 'Alstonism' has many antecedents, not just in the early and mid-'80s. As Ken Inglis's history of the ABC demonstrates, there has barely been a time when Labor and Liberal have failed to attack, damage and demonise the ABC.[5]

Radio networks are still, twenty years on, the main place where the ABC maintains its charter commitment to the arts. Arguably, arts discussion fits better into the bed of ABC radio's staple mainly-talk programs, with their talk-back sessions and talk-based features. How much arts-related news, announcements, talk and interview, for instance, occurs on the regional stations? My sense, as I move around New South Wales, is that local arts events, visiting writers, exhibitions and craft shows get welcome air play: if the local writer's centre or gallery or librarian sets up the link, the day-time and often evening talk-host is keen to talk. Similarly, while many listeners interested in the arts might not be regular Metro (major city) consumers, a surprising amount of art talk, art news and art commentary is scattered across these stations. In the last 24 hours of my scattered Metro listening I heard a film reviewer, an etymologist, a book reviewer and a curator; but then, living where I do (and perhaps depending on rural wind direction or other cosmological influences) I double-dip and get the remote Brisbane ABC, and even regional Queensland, better than I do the closer Sydney. Certainly, it is striking that Liz Jacka's report was not discussed at all on the coast-to-coast RN, but was discussed by James Valentine on the Sydney

Metro station. Were RN producers instructed by management *not* to mention it because RN was one of the report's main areas of contention?

RN continues to carry a number of arts-related programs. Julie Copeland's *Sunday Morning*, much of Alan Saunders' *Comfort Zone* or composer Andrew Ford's Saturday morning *Music Show* are invaluable interview material (and, in Ford's case, music clips) with arts specialists, with writers at work in the arts or music or design areas—and often have extended interviews with, for instance, performers, curators and composers. While many of us are still asking why RN's coverage of visual arts has never been extensive, Julie Copeland includes a craft-based or visual arts-based interview in her 'Maker' segment.

There is a weekly poetry program, produced in and broadcast from Adelaide. There is no poetry magazine, however, for new and unsolicited work. Nor is there very much critical discussion of poetry, which is not surprising since there is now very little informed critical talk of any kind on the station, whether of books or theatre or music, or newer forms of performance work or music. In fact, the voices of writers and artists and critics and filmmakers and composers and arts-related theorists and philosophers are scarcely audible anywhere, *unless* in those snappy, magazine-style short interviews. Similarly, researched or specialist critical pieces have all but vanished from the arts area. Why? The sometimes awkwardly-delivered science commentary, *Occam's Razor*, is justifiably one of RN's most popular programs. Edited versions of entire lectures, seminars, public talks are broadcast on science programs, on talks-unit programs like *Background Briefing*, on *Late-Night Live*, occasionally on *The Media Report* and on the excellent religious programs. Why not in the arts areas, too?

Have the arts been singled out? Have writers, painters, media artists, online artists, dramatists, actors and actresses, critics, arts academics, arts administrators, dancers, choreographers, video makers, composers and craft artists talked themselves under the media table? Informed debate and opinion are acceptable on air in all intellectual areas—except the arts. Perhaps some concession has been handed to popular culture debate, but even here there is very little detail, very little studied response. Theological or political ideas, or stock market reports can be presented whole, but an art object only in bits, by sleight of hand and in cunning asides. Why? From whom has the assumption come that audiences loathe hearing writers, actors, painters, photographers, poets, sculptors, dancers, media artists, sounds artists, composers and designers? The 2000 Saatchi and Saatchi report pointed out that for every Australian who is not interested in information about or access to the arts, there is another who is. The report also pointed out, predictably enough, that many Australians felt that despite their interest in the arts, the arts were 'not really for them'. The arts remain somewhat out of reach or removed. Is it the listeners who have herded themselves into this intimidated, negative view of art and literature, or is it mainly ABC Radio's recently-appointed management?

3

There are two cultures in the ABC: the managerial and the intellectual/artistic. They seldom meet.[6]

G iven its current funding and its current policies, the national broadcaster will have great difficulty fulfilling even a minimal program of intelligent, cutting-edge arts-based programming. Liz Jacka inclines to the view that the negative, intimidated view is mainly a management view. Focussing her remarks on TV more than on radio or online, Jacka identifies as symptomatic of the editorial problem the policy of 'arts by stealth'. Jacka is seeking to explain why, for example, the production of TV documentaries in the arts has been reduced in recent years:

> In the last five years ABC-TV has undergone a definite change of direction in relation to arts programming. The explicit strategy espoused by Director of Television, Sandra Levy, is 'arts by stealth', seemingly sharing the view of ABC radio that the word 'arts' scares people, although the words 'science', 'law', 'media' and 'religion' do not. So arts will be smuggled in via other timeslots [...] but it won't be there in prime time in an identified arts slot.[7]

In other words, the arts will only be mentioned in passing. A comment about an arts event will be like covert product placement in a movie shot: you will never quite notice it. The radio equivalent of this 'stealth' is RN's reliance on a glancing, snapshot way of dealing with arts talk: such talk often seems not to be about the thing, the work, the process of making the work, and it rarely emerges as part of a critically informed talk or a well thought-out and many-sided presentation.

All over a station like RN, for instance, there are tell-tale signs of a drifting anxiousness about the reception of art and literature. It is symptomatic that the literary program *Books and Writing* now mainly plays agreeable, off-the-cuff interviews. It has a very high proportion of overseas writers on the international festival circuit. Its brief is no longer critical or part of the wider reviewing culture of newspapers and magazines; nor does it give any special emphasis to local writers. If *Books and Writing* sometimes risks degenerating into standardised literary 'chat' with Edinburgh traffic noise in the background, what to say of the sadly mis-titled week-night program *The Deep End*? Only the most benign would say that RN has yet got this program right. Here the limits of relying on spontaneous talk and a limited range of permissible topic areas become embarrassingly plain. Steer away from what's historical, from painting, from anything classical in either literary or musical terms, anything about experimental art practice, anything relating to the ideas and theoretical contexts of contemporary art, and what is left? Fail to grasp what the new generation of young Australians is doing in music or media art or poetry or dance and why should you attract the younger audience? One difficulty is that popular culture is not really a 'young' term: it's academic, a media studies and a cultural studies construct. If RN wants to make an exciting program which explores the local and international range of writings and image-based work which crosses over between history, cultural studies, media theory and the newer forms of fiction, photography, media art, sound art, innovative musics and online art, it should do so. There is a wealth of Australian work. *The Deep End* does not live up to its avowed—excellent—aim of exploring 'what's happening in the arts in Australia and overseas, bringing listeners the latest ideas'. The shadows of earlier arts talk programs, which relied on a wide range of specialists, hang heavily over this program's unruffled waters. Clearly, this year's new presenter/producer is trying to define the show's role and strengthen its content. But it remains very reliant on film talk and pop culture comment. It still has to make a splash.

Paradoxically, Jacka probably overestimates how much stealth there has been in the undermining of arts programs on radio. The budgets which allowed producers to commission writers and composers, employ actors or buy already-produced new pieces have been diminished in very obvious ways. This applies equally to drama, to music, to audio works, to literary and art reviews, to the commissioning of independently-made features. The problem is not primarily that program slots like the stereo play or the audio arts and innovative feature show, *The Listening Room*, have been canned. The fixed program slot is not the problem. Indeed, there may well be good reasons to develop and change these formats and the kind of work which is presented in them. The program's name is not at issue; the renewal of editorial aims and content is a good thing. But the absence of a budget to produce new work is a problem.

In short, there can be no subtle relocation of the work of new playwrights, audio artists, composers and feature makers across ABC-FM or RN, if less and less of such work is going to be made. How much new drama, new acoustic work, new features and radiophonic documentaries will be made in the future no-one seems able to say. There are also no guidelines as to how, or whether, the ABC intends to engage in sound production (acoustic, musical, arts documentary) which substantially involves external artists. There has been a serious weakening of the commitment at ABC Radio to the culture—and the policy—of commissioning writers and composers. Arguably, there is insufficient money for such a commitment. Less arguably, what we are witnessing is the destruction of a whole tradition of long-lived engagement with the world of arts and letters.

It is hard to over-emphasise the loss, a loss that will be bitterly felt in the future. Who will commission the young media artists, the new and emerging writers who do not work in traditional formats, the new generation of composers? ABC Radio networks have had a key creative, sculpting role in relation to emerging areas of the arts. The ABC has been a leading national agency in the fashioning of our literary, dramatic and musical culture. There might no longer be the will, the policy or the commissioning budget to maintain that role, but the necessity of such a role has not disappeared. Listeners interested in the range of classical and contemporary literatures, in traditional and non-traditional arts and in the wide range of contemporary and classical musics can already hear the 'thinness' of the main networks: too much scripted and produced program material is repeated; programs like *The Deep End* sound under-researched, shallow art talk replacing engaging discussion. ABC Classic-FM has increased its broadcasts of recorded concerts, but the work tends to be far too mainstream while attention to Australian music and contemporary music has been de-emphasised. A little acoustic work occurs very late at night. But in too many areas, only already-commissioned work is proceeding, and tight budget constraints are limiting further commissions. There appear to be no plans for the longer future. The ABC's international reputation as an innovative commissioner and maker of feature work from local and overseas writers, artists and composers is fast eroding.[8]

The decline of specialist knowledges, expertise and production capacity in the arts at the ABC is a national concern. It cannot be passed off as a mere after-effect of a management strategy to do with chasing ratings. It cannot be forgiven as an 'inevitable' result of Federal government funding hostility. It is like saying that we will approve the running down of the Australian

National Library as a major specialist institution in the national cultural life. Or that we tolerate the closing of the State and National Art Galleries. The specialist media-based creative knowledges and expertise which form the core strength of the ABC are key areas which link creative work—the profile, the innovative richness of Australian art, writing, drama and critical culture—with a wider, and potentially a mass, audience. Once that expertise goes, once all the production capacity is turned into chat manufactured for 'light' or slightly less 'light' consumption, once the ABC loses an engaged and imaginative editorial role in relation to the arts, it is not clear to me that such expertise etc. can simply be hired as required.

Current ABC policies appear set against maintaining the specialist producers, the areas of knowledge, the technical skill and the commissioning budgets necessary for the ABC to have what was earlier termed a significantly creative, editorial presence in Australian culture. Signs of that decline are everywhere on TV and radio. Even the excellent online portal, *The Space*, needs updating and development: staff positions were lost and the portal is frozen. ABC-TV may be chasing the impossible, success to rival the commercial channels, at the cost of losing its primary role. To give a final example: today ABC Radio would probably not consider producing a play by Shakespeare, Chekhov, Williamson or White. It still has the expertise, but no longer the money or the time-slot.

4

... the act of critically reading with one's own eyes and ears requires a leap of speculation—informed speculation, but speculation nonetheless.[9]

It's Thursday night and I am doggedly watching ABC-TV. Why doggedly? Like many people I know, I am no longer a sustained, night-after-night viewer of television. For one thing, I'm too busy. For another, I mix and match various forms of broadcast, replay, pay-TV and online media. Of course, I watch ABC news, though over the last year or so I, like others, have become wary of the issue of self-censorship in relation to Liberal and National Party pressure on the channel. In a way, I am a relatively 'professional' viewer, conscious of how items are ordered, time and attention allocated to various viewpoints, issues prioritised and emphasised. These days, like many others, I regularly channel-hop between SBS and the commercial channels, to see how differently the news is structured on other networks. My 'news picture' comes from this contrastive viewing, from selected newspaper reading the following day, listening to ABC Radio, occasionally dipping into overseas weeklies. Besides, like many others, I regularly go to web sources, mostly international ones, to get either breaking or background information.

I mention this complex question of whether, and how, a station awakens an implicit involvement, a trust-filled engagement because it has some bearing on how all the other sorts of program which are not news and commentary are viewed. On this particular Thursday evening I am looking at *Fireflies*, a new drama series which as the weeks pass looks seriously bogged on a bush track half-way between *SeaChange* and *Police Rescue*. (I've not been a dedicated viewer and have missed parts of the story, though that doesn't really seem to matter.) *Mondo Thingo*, an arts show—but that might not be the right term—will follow later.

Fireflies has been advertised over recent days as a particularly appropriate series for those of us who are glutted with reality television. Presumably this promotion is designed to suggest *Fireflies* will be watched by sprightly, station-hopping viewers who regularly watch reality shows on commercial networks. Perhaps it is to do with the fact that another network's restaurant reality show (which I have, I admit, flicked across to on other Thursdays) is in direct competition. As must be the case for many viewers, these pre-set ideas about who is watching *Fireflies* do not strike me as being specially acute, though I am conscious of an implied pattern of viewing, an implied audience. After all, many of *Fireflies*' characters are in their mid- to late-40s, while many of the program's assumptions about country life reek of 1970s 'hippie' values. There are also younger actors and more contemporary themes, some of which have a somewhat ill-defined connection with the bush fire brigade's role in a country community. Yet somehow, we seem to be being told, this program needs its audience to be a few years younger. There is a peculiar, and noticeable, disjunction here between potential peer-group sympathy with the themes and characters of the series and the claim that '20-somethings' or '30-somethings' might enjoy it. I doubt that enough of them do.[10]

The truth is the promo hypes up a not-very-good episode. This particular episode is close to 'reality' only in the sense that the location has hijacked the script. Set in the New South Wales bush, with many scenes shot outdoors, the ferocious temperatures of the summer just gone seem to have become the episode's over-riding background theme. There are lots of fine, heat-stressed actors, tinnie in hand, flopping into broken-down chairs outside rough-hewn shacks and caravans. Perhaps the problem, however, is not the heat, and the constant, enervating reference made to it. The problem is aesthetic, filmic, structural. For a show which takes things at a reasonably slow pace, there are too many themes and sub-themes. A quick review of this globally-warmed episode would, for instance, have to include family problems, two or three versions of generational warfare, the fires, relationship issues, jealousy, teenage love, whether to have a child or not, an ex-boyfriend's fatal heroin overdose, some nefarious accounting, the suspicion of drug-dealing, rural snobbery towards sea-change newcomers … By no means exhaustive—I haven't mentioned the property-developers—this list is long enough, however, to cause one to ask: when is enough enough? When do enough tense interaction, enough terse dialogue, enough shots of cars arriving and departing, enough beer guts and singlets, heads popping through kitchen doors and footsteps on the verandah, add up to a series of scenes that work properly as television drama? Social and community life in the bush has become a firestorm of issues and problems: but not enough is going on visually, in the shot, in the angle, or in the actors' lines. Besides, if *Fireflies* offers a snapshot of a not-too-far-inland country community—and, moreover, *better* than reality—what kind of picture is it taking? Is it *SeaChange* five years on? In which case, be warned. Or is it the hippies at the back of Byron Bay thirty years on? In which case, don't go there.

Why discuss *Fireflies*, at all, in an essay about the ABC and the arts? First, of course, it is an example of 'new television drama'. Indeed, it is the *only* significant drama on the ABC at present. Correction: because, given the near-total demise of performance and drama on ABC Radio, with the exception of a 23-minute radio-piece on Sunday afternoons, *Fireflies* is *the only significant local drama the national broadcaster is broadcasting at present on any of its networks*. That fact is significant, not to say breathtaking. What has happened, for instance, to the notion that the ABC might offer a range of different types of local drama? What, too, has happened to scripted, serial comedy? Middle-of-the-road taste might, at a pinch, be catered for by the co-produced rural series *Fireflies*, but there is no classic drama—Shakespeare, Ibsen, Miller, Pinter, Shepard—and there is no series showcasing contemporary Australian playwrights. On sound-alone channels, RN is carrying no experimental theatre, ABC Classic-FM is carrying no recently commissioned stereo theatre. True, RN is carrying repeats of already broadcast audio features, which often have acted components. Of longer, more complex work, there is nothing—other, that is, than *Fireflies*.

The particular problems, different from those of *Fireflies'* TV context, which beset the relationship between contemporary Australian art practice and ABC radio will be looked at later. For now, I want to stay with Thursday night. Was I, I wondered, simply the victim of a category mistake? Was I, or the program, in the wrong category? I had been watching with the wrong expectations. The drama I hoped might challenge the orthodoxy—the conventions of this sort of television series, the standard relationship between real life and documentary drama, the way the bush is represented—was not aspiring to do that. The truth is that *Fireflies* is not awful, but it is only a tad more interesting than ordinary. It will dub effortlessly into Brazilian or German—indeed, suit any overseas market. It breaks no boundaries. But then, again, was I the victim of a category mistake in another sense? Should I not have looked to 'legitimate drama' for my more challenging moment of television? Perhaps I had the wrong genre. What about *Stand Up!*, the comedy series that also screens on Thursday nights? That is certainly 'performance'; it is 'local' and it does break boundaries. Or looking ahead, in the coming week there would be *Live at the Basement* and a documentary about at the Australian Opera going outback with Puccini. Further, if I were looking for work which broadly supports performance and drama, why had I simply turned to something local? That, too, may have been a category mistake. For instance, although programs like *Taggart* and *Monarch of the Glen* are not Australian-made, they are examples of the ABC presenting drama. Besides, in a pop cultural way, these series can also have unintended benefits where local work is concerned: hardly a local production, *The Bill*, for instance, has spawned its own Australian poetic subgenre in which poets create cut-up poems that borrow scenarios from this popular, long-running British drama.[11] There is nothing straightforward about what counts and what doesn't count as a contribution to local arts.

The issues became increasingly interesting to think about as the evening wore on. What sort of parameters might there be to an ABC drama series? What sorts of ideas about writing and television might it accommodate? The current holder of the New South Wales Writers Fellowship is a dramatist who makes use of detailed documentary research in her work, blending such materials into her play scripts, making use of verbatim accounts of what real people say and do as well as of historical and contemporary documents. Her work draws upon a very lively contemporary form of film and theatre which breaks down boundaries between real life, television and recorded depictions of real life, blending and reworking these elements into what we see on stage or camera. There is nothing inaccessible about these innovative techniques by which leading writers explore the relationship between everyday speech, everyday perceptions, recordings, documents, oral histories, photographs, film footage and filmic conventions: they are, as this example suggests, often the materials writers use directly when they come to write lively, modern drama. There is no suggestion here that there exists a set path to follow in the making of innovative drama, and that the creators of *Fireflies* should have followed it. My point is simply that, in Australia at the moment, there is a lively, technically innovating context for creating 'real life' drama—the current official writer of the state where I live is a leading practitioner.

Clearly, the ABC's aims for a series like *Fireflies* sit miles away, on the other side of the mountain range, from considerations such as these. The result is that someone—a hip 20-something, a moderately well-informed adult in his or her mid-40s—who sees new movies and the latest theatre will be disappointed, and someone who isn't watching the Cohn brothers, or *Bowling for Columbine*, or hasn't just seen Nicolas Philibert's *To Be and To Have*, a close-up portrait of French country life seen through the prism of a one-room country school, is not getting anything new, or any new idea of how good new films and drama can be.[12] This viewer may not instantly know *why* his or her experience is a let-down, but will guess all the same that it is. There do exist real opportunities for exploring the relation between the documentary reality of a rural New South Wales community and the nature of a TV series, as the above examples demonstrate, but *Fireflies* hasn't explored them. Where it gets close to reality—for example, in its acknowledgement of the serious heroin problem in many country towns, or of how impoverished country life can be, both socially and financially—these ideas have not seeded any new approach to form or a challenging visual idiom. They have been left as grist for a conventional scripting and shooting process. Clearly, my expectations overload an otherwise harmless series. It would not matter if the ABC had something else on offer.[13]

No less evidently, whatever the mixed messages about the series' target audience, few of us are going to watch such a show primarily *because* we identify with an implied fed-up reality-show audience or with either of the implied age groups. To take the crudest markers: nothing about the show suggests that watching it is smart or trendy. Or that the issues it raises are indispensable coffee conversation. Or that since only 20- and 30-somethings *do* watch it, the rest of us had better catch up. The paradox is that, in terms of ratings, I am probably an ideal constituent of this series' demographic. I live for a good part of the year in one of the out-of-town locations where many of *Fireflies'* external shots are taken. I have a long-standing interest in regional arts, and in acknowledging how Australia looks from regional standpoints. I mention the heroin problem in country towns because, together with unemployment, there is a serious problem of drug abuse in the town I drive to for my shopping. I can identify the local sources of some of *Fireflies'* more substantial themes. It could all be so much closer to 'what it's really like out there'. It could have so much more *reality*, and much more exciting television.

5

... kitsch, destined for those who, insensible to the values of genuine culture, are hungry nevertheless for the diversion that only culture of some sort can provide ...[14]

There's no need to take up much more space on the rest of that Thursday evening. *Mondo Thingo* knows how exciting it is only too well, rarely pausing from saying so. Comedian and former breakfast host, Amanda Keller, anchors a show in which most of the content is chosen for its mix of trash and flash. Little is memorable. Ironic one-liners abound. Keller herself is interesting, but the show heavily parodies TV arts-show mannerisms, overdoes close-ups of the host, an exaggerated emphasis on talk and on funky cuts to insert feature items. The joke dies after a few minutes. According to the ABC website *Mondo Thingo* provides 'news and pop culture essentials'. Fast-paced, *Thingo* is presumably trying to match its risky claim to be 'distilling the whirlwind of pop culture hype and desperation'. This week's episode is irksome: there is a real difficulty to do with whether the scenes are about laughing or sneering. Trivial comments about *Willy Wonka* enter a whirlwind mix to do with reflections on *Basic Instinct*, and a pretentious item on so-called culture-jamming. In case any of us had not got wind of the phrase a while ago, culture-jamming, it transpires, is more or less spray-painting and graffiti, with a bit of digital tail-spin thrown in: frightfully earnest, a brief feature interviews a couple of definitely 30-something Americans who are trying to block out some very selective instances of commercial hype.

Nowhere in the program is there any pressure to extend any of the ideas discussed, or make it interesting. After all, aren't lots of other pop-cultural media activities a kind of culture-jamming? The term can also include the undermining of celebrities, scandal-mongering, desecration. Like 'the royals', Posh and Beckham, I reckon, have been pretty effectively 'culture-jammed' recently, by the Murdoch press. So have indigenous Australians, by the current Federal government. The problem with *Thingo*'s sneers and self-conscious silliness is that they do not allow anything to happen, anything which might connect with or challenge serious thinking. An hour or so into 'our ABC' on this particular evening, it is clear that a much more deeply-formed cyclonic system than

Mondo Thingo has blown away serious attention to the arts or lively commitment to supporting drama. If culture-jamming is a topical issue, then kitsch-oriented programs like *Mondo Thingo* are probably doing the blocking.[15]

A thin handful of other arts programs are screened on ABC-TV. The half-hour *Message Stick* has an indigenous focus and often talks about art. Jonathan Biggins' *Critical Mass* brings together a brief forum, dealing regularly with film—currently the predominant performing art-form on both television and radio. It gets a day-time repeat, but a last-thing-on-Sunday-night time-slot says much about the expected reception of intelligent talk on the channel. Perhaps, now that the ABC has announced its 'coup'—after a mere eighteen years—of poaching David Stratton and Margaret Pomeranz from SBS, *Critical Mass* will live up to the meaning of its name and disintegrate into some new formation.

Personal likes and dislikes, of course, are not the issue. The difficulty is that very little of this programming, no matter how well-mapped in terms of likely demographics or popular viewing times, makes its content essential viewing. Essential, that is, because something—some sense of the new, some moment of suspense, some feeling of tapping into what s/he needs to know—*insists* that the viewer or listener not miss the next edition, the next episode. Who will go back to these programs, wish to remember them, see them again? Who will put their time-slot in the mental diary? Who cares enough about what will be blown in by the next breeze of that pop-culture wind, or whether what might occur in Lost River actually does? Given that critical reviewing generally makes less of an impact, whether in papers or on television, how does the ABC's carefully-selected team of critical specialists seek to reverse that trend in their discussions of sometimes good, sometimes middling films or books? The problem, it must be added, is not that the programs are clumsily made or unprofessional. They're not, but neither are they exciting, nor do they surprise; and they carry insufficient authority, whether as path-breaking examples of the genre or as innovatively researched and written. Nor do they seem to know what to do with this lack of a capacity for, or of a reaching out towards, an authoritative place. They don't make fun, for example, or satirise. They just occur; they are part of the station's audience-producing product. They do not divide the kids from the adults, the sheep from the goats.

Despite being about viewpoint and critical opinion—and perhaps we should acknowledge that it *is* an example, a lonely example, of an arts discussion program on the ABC—even *Critical Mass* does not escape from the environing arts blandness. Jonathan Biggins is fine as the anchor of *Critical Mass*, but the panellists seem to have been asked to pretend they have met several times before on an arts committee. They are far too anxious to agree before they disagree. Throughout the arts programs, a big concern is about not upsetting anybody, not stretching the boundaries or sounding out of sorts. ABC drama and arts programming is getting depressingly close to what science broadcaster, Robyn Williams, satirised a few years ago as 'Chatter TV'. Close, I stress. Williams was thinking of Oprah and an audience of 'wrinklies' (his phrase), while the ABC seems to be thinking of a few poorly-identified '30-somethings'.[16]

This hesitant re-positioning of the potential audience—in itself a defensible aim—is not the only cause of unadventurous, creatively weak arts programming. Other broader strategies are leading to practices which disengage from the best creative work. Thus, ABC-TV appears to have realised that if it cannot draw sustained and specific attention to its programming—if, in short, it cannot keep drawing in and drawing back adventurous viewers who want to look at new, well-made and well-funded programs— then it must consolidate. It must focus on core ratings. It must focus on its place in league-table of the 'Top 50 TV Programs': for example, one week in April its highest-rated show, *The Bill*, occupied 28th spot. It must not offend or risk losing, even momentarily, what audience it still attracts. Apparently, this might happen, were it to broadcast programs on visual artists or contemporary music, a controversial critics' show, or season of gay-related movies or regionally-based dramas from new writers. In short, if the criteria and the implied viewing area are not 'lowest common' denominator, then they are nonetheless restrictively 'common' denominator.

True, viewing and listening have changed in recent years. Twenty years ago the ABC engagement with arts and culture set what it was doing aside from what other agencies, such as publishers, newspapers or arts organisations, were doing. This is less true today: the culture market is global, cultural interests are less localised. Information about, experiences to do with, the arts come from a variety of sources, whether from the hugely expanded newspaper supplements, or from festivals, block-buster art shows, regional arts events and so on. While none of these events have much individual impact on viewing and listening practices, but together they add up to a context for broadcasting differently motivated from the 'classical' rather BBC-ish idea enshrined in the ABC charter—I mean those ideas about the broadcast medium's specialist role in fostering, in nurturing, or in giving access to those without access. Similarly the challenge is not only to do with the shifting viewing habits and interests of the younger audience. For, if we return to the example of multimedia, it is not just the '20-somethings' and the '30-somethings' who are now on the web as much as they are tuned in to television: a very large section of all television and radio audiences are online literate.

True, too, the circumstances in which the ABC can become a key player in the arts communities of Australia have changed radically over the last two decades. Back in the mid-'80s, I was fascinated by that day-to-day sense of an ABC community open to a wide variety of writers, artists and program makers: this was probably more a phenomenon of ABC Radio than TV. RN was a carefully selected and very high-level arts laboratory, where 'insiders' and 'outsiders' combined their talents. Radio studios are, I suppose, likely to be places which draw in a large number of writers, talkers, singers and actors: such is the trade. Is there a contemporary digital equivalent of this form of (to use a rather hefty term) cultural interaction? For that was what it was *in parvo*. Like a strange sort of electronic theatre company, not all of whose members were professional actors, the show went on, every day and every night. It worked as an entity. It was (to use two more professionalised, hefty words) an excellent model of networking and collaboration. Is there a digital version of this? In asking that, let me repeat that I have no desire to go back, to try to reconstitute a summer of enlightened swallows. In truth, even at the time, RN struck me as being time-frozen in what I think of as its 'Ithacan' moment. The house, in other words, was filled with suitors—writers, broadcasters, performers. The tapestry of sounds and words was being woven and unwoven day by day, night by night. To a degree, nobody was really getting what they wanted: a secure audience, fame, lots of money, sustained and credible reviews, your name in lights. And to launch a brilliant career it was understood you would have to leave the island. Was it enough? Nobody asked the question. Meanwhile, as the palace of sounds and ideas, voices and words, began year by year to fall apart, no-one really noticed, not for a while. There was no expectation, or need to expect, an Odysseus to appear on the road from the port.

But all of that said, there is one fact which remains as true today as it did then: if you do not find a contemporary way to broadcast the work of the country's best artists to the nation, performers and writers, all you are doing is telling your audience (the nation) that they shall not have access to it.

6

She sat and looked at the screen. It was compelling to her, real enough to withstand the circumstance of nothing going on. It thrived on the circumstance.[17]

Despite the enormous influence of electronic, digital and, more generally, recording media on our everyday lives, there are surprisingly few historical accounts of what listening to or watching media feels like. There is an enormous amount of theory, there is considerable statistical research based on surveys and there is a deal of history and informed commentary on policy and government issues. But there are very few reliable accounts of what, for example, it was like to sit in a room in the 1930s and listen to radio, and not many more accounts of the later experience of portable transistors in the 1950s. Not many story writers, similarly, have written about the car radio, one of the main forms of listening in our time, particularly in Australia.

Surprisingly, the same can be said of television-viewing and video streaming. Arguably a few more accounts of television-watching than of radio-listening have found their way into fiction. Yoel Ravid in Amos Oz's *To Know a Woman* watches television with a memorable kind of vague focus, while the Israeli secret service put him out to pasture. Don DeLillo's *The Body Artist* makes marvellously evocative use of video-streamed imaging coming through a television terminal as part of an environmental installation work. True, radios and television monitors turn up in film scenes, but there are few times when the engaged moment of viewing and listening is reflected on. Exceptionally, it is the gramophone which has provoked a number of significant writers to think about the experience of listening. One of these, the poet Rainer Maria Rilke, writing just after the First World War, developed the bizarre idea of taking recordings directly from any groove or contour including those of the human cranium, much as the needle rides over the old-fashioned record. 'Is there any contour which one could not complete in this way and then experience it [...] in another field of sense?', he asks.[18] Later in the twentieth century, essayist Roland Barthes writes with metaphoric intensity about the connections he sensed when listening to both live and recorded music, caught between a deeply inward embodiment of acoustic sensation and the stereophonic sound of the late 1960s. All such listening to music is, he says, 'steeped in desire'.[19]

These and similar accounts remind us how easy it is to forget what is happening when we listen or watch. For instance, RN recently broadcast a very memorable event, and for a moment began to reinstate that idea that the station's engagement with the arts and writing was indeed essential listening. Someone, inventively, thinking laterally, decided to build a raft of ideas between various magazine programs, choosing to focus elements in each of them around the theme of Greek influence. Greek philosophy, the Greek inheritance in the broad historical panoply of the Anglo-American culture many of us share, the Greek inheritance in language as evidenced, for instance, by words like 'panoply' and, together with that, the special Greekness of multicultural Australian culture—all these threads wove and interwove across a series of different programs. Other programs carried Greek poetry, Seferis, Elitis and Ritsos. The Sydney poet Antigone Kefala was one of the readers. There was a program on Greek popular music traditions. Hippocrates and Galen were both on *All in the Mind*. There were references to the current Olympics, and to Lord Elgin's theft of the Acropolis's relief statuary. The unifying theme was not too insistently pressed. The links with the news around the Greek elections and the preparations for the Olympics were handled carefully and unobtrusively.

Once the radio was on, I found myself continuing to listen to programs, wondering what Greek item would come next. I didn't catch a play by Aeschylus or Aristophanes: were there the means and program space to produce one? The website announces the broadcast in May of a play, by Alan Hancock, on a modernised Homeric theme. There was a sense that the station was setting out to engage the audience and, importantly, to build relationships across and between areas of interest. It was not just 'audio talk', wallpaper designed for a given demographic. It allowed program makers and announcers to extend connections, between cosmology and Pythagoras, between jazz and Kazanzakis, between Rembetica and readings from Symposium. This month of 'Greek Imprints', as it was called, was not arts by indirection or disguise, but arts by networking, nuance, clever composition and juxtaposition. There was no need to hide or 're-package' the work, pretending it wasn't what it was. Once the various items were allowed to speak to each other, the programming's overall impact built and built. The effect was of listening to a lively, interestingly haphazard form of curating. A contribution from Channel 2—say, a series of Greek movies or movies on Greek themes—would have made the package perfect. Probably the time-lines for buying and forward-planning in television are too difficult to manipulate. But some program or programs which networked between the two media of television and sound would have been intriguing and inventive.

ABC Radio has broadcast a number of other curated, long-term profiles of this sort—a world historical one at the time of the millennium, for example—and they provide some indication that a station like RN can successfully focus on specific issues and genres, and on specific areas of knowledge, intellectual achievement and art practice, as a way of attracting and building audiences. Why not more such curated events? Why shouldn't the ABC creatively editorialise, inventively overviewing ideas about and from arts? If we think locally, why not a month devoted to the city-versus-bush theme, or the indigenous contribution to Australian culture? If we think globally, the themes of the contribution of science to art and vice-versa, or of the environment and the arts, come to mind—the list of topical, lively ideas which are relevant to the everyday mind-set of Australians is very long. Shift the focus and put a contemporary philosophical 'cluster' at the centre: the major themes to do with contemporary approaches to mind and body, medical, genetic, cognitive and 'consciousness theory'. Why not look beyond Australia and think of an 'Americana' month, a month of American influences: everyone from Tom Schieffer to Marshall Mathers could be in it.

Of course, the point here is not that these sorts of curated seasons are a programming solution to the challenge of how to entrap and entrance the curious viewer or listener. Their attraction would diminish as soon as the editorial device became obvious; different channels and different networks would have less or no involvement, depending on the nature of the project and so on. The same factors of maximal and minimal times for audiences apply as readily to these interlinked program ideas as to stand-alone programs. The point is simpler: viewers' and listeners' viewing and listening habits begin to engage as soon as the ABC itself engages in a lively and innovative way with ideas in themselves, and with new program ideas. The arts (creative work such as plays, films, music, stories) and discussion around the arts (features on composers and painters, discussions on experimental arts, on social and theoretical issues associated with the arts) have an obvious role to play in any broadly creative editorial approach which puts the emphasis on ideas and on direct engagement with the audience, not just on ratings and the manufacture of statistically-defined audiences.

In part, too, there is a real opportunity for outreach and networking in a creatively editorialised, art-work oriented approach to production. All too often, the ABC looks like an isolated producer, doing its own work partly in tandem with others and partly not. To go back to the earlier mainly radio example: as soon as an idea like 'Greek Imprints' occurs, there is an opportunity for the community to engage; there is an opportunity for publishers, community organisations, cultural organisations, theatre groups, dance groups, arts festivals (two of which are listed on the 'Greek Imprints'website), arts administrators, regional communities. They can respond, contribute and take part. In short, the ABC engages across the wider cultural and arts landscape. The airwaves become both transmitters and receivers. This initiative, that project, that series, that film and book series become part of a wider world, identified at a series of levels which are not exclusively those of the broadcast, the rating, the limited moment of exposure. Instead, a creative, and critically informative, space opens up in the air. The many interesting ways in which the ABC already links programs with publications, CDs and tapes are evidence that this is already happening. And across the distinct, but converging platforms of sound, image and multimedia, viewers, listeners and web visitors have, potentially at least, a range of different ways of engaging with the material. Furthermore, this viewer/ listener/visitor might be someone who goes to galleries, plays, local community events, the school play and the community arts event.

For what the 'Greek Imprints' example teases out is the way in which a media object is received, how it is 'read', how it has impact, how it relates to the audience. The example is, in short, more to do with the sense of excitement which momentarily overtook the airwaves and the reasons for that excitement, than with offering programming advice to ABC producers and managers. At the same time, my example is about recognising that if there is a landscape of production and reception practices in which media, and the media representation of art, will flourish, there is also a complex landscape of listening and viewing practices. Listening and viewing flow into, and out of, the overall environment of the ways in which Australians engage with the arts. What the ABC is doing is not isolated from what anybody else is doing—neither in terms of production nor in terms of consumption and audience attention.

The ABC was, and is, one of the few media organisations which have tried to respond to and develop that complex of listening and viewing practices. All the more tragic, then, that more of its programs are not available streamed or downloaded. To take an obvious instance, when does ABC-FM get through the 'hot' potato-vine infested thicket of contract and copyright questions which prevents most of its programming being available at *The Space*?

Online services release program makers from the constraint of depending on real-time audiences only: programs can be saved, archived, temporarily downloaded. Visual programs are not isolated from sound-alone programs. Text, publishing, electronic publishing are integral to the way such a multimedia site can be read. The formal properties of drama, painterly or photo image, shorter films, spoken word, visual and recited poem, book-reading, abstract and experimental art work lend themselves to cross-platform modes of delivery. Contemporary forms of media and media-based performance art would seem especially well placed on the site: *The Space* could even stream the environmental work which so uncannily disturbs the peaceful interior of the northern California house at the centre of Don DeLillo's novel, *The Body Artist*.

Many ABC producers are keenly aware of the possible interplay between web broadcast, electronic publishing and electronic archiving, when combined with the positioning of programs on real-time channels such as a radio network or a TV station. It offers a dazzling opportunity for cleverly structured approaches to cultural and arts subject matter. To a degree, such an interplay between web-access and real-time viewing and listening reflects the multi-levelled way in which we are all beginning to respond to media. Like many people today, I 'sit down to watch' television less and less frequently. When I do, watching and listening occur in frequently interrupted blocks of time. That moment of excitement has to persuade me to stay with a longer program. Or it can be deferred and experienced archivally in a webcast. Mixed live and web broadcasts and re-shaped ABC arts programming within the format of a sound and image electronic museum offer multi-levelled access. A mix of networked, archived and broadband broadcasting would then also become one of the convergent platforms which could genuinely benefit the arts by bringing a new and different sort of viewer and listener into the ambit of the work. The younger audience might not require the cajoling, or embarrassed gesturing, that seem currently to afflict the ABC's approach to creative work. This mix might also offer new ways to network with theatre and performance groups, with media artists, and other community and professionally-based arts groups. No doubt there are major opportunities for publicity and greater opportunities for commercialisation. There must be huge frustration within the ABC about the way in which the organisation's capacity to engage with— indeed, play a vital, shaping role in the development of—new media formats has been blocked. The present moment of dull, enforced freeze has set back many aspects of the ABC, including the Corporation's support for the arts and their capacity to maintain and attract audiences. This cannot be said strongly enough.

7

*Our weapons were
our instruments
made from timber
and steel
we never yielded to
conformity.[20]*

ABC Radio's traditionally widespread involvement in the commissioning, making and producing of new work in music, drama, performance and acoustic arts has been diminished.[21] Elsewhere in the Corporation, a mainstreaming, ratings-related approach to programming has been simplistically confused with a distrust of the ability of arts programs and directly commissioned new works to attract audiences or viewers. New initiatives look lonely and are supported by very little incisive, widely articulated policy about how the ABC's role in the arts might be maintained, promoted or expanded. A mainstreaming, 'common-denominator' approach to arts programming has taken over the ABC's only television channel. Not surprisingly, this has not brought about any new arts magazine programs, significant documentary series on the arts, sudden flourishing of dance film, seasons of music-theatre simulcasts or of new Australian drama. There seems little likelihood of either well-known literary writers or young, emerging playwrights or emergent film makers or even a young comedy team finding a welcome at the ABC. Were an extra-terrestrial to take this last week's programming as a random sample, it would conclude that contemporary theatre and film arts impact on the ABC, if at all, merely in review segments. The visitor would also see that there has been inadequate nurturing of the initial signs of a sensitive cross-platform approach to multimedia broadcasting, which might benefit the arts generally and some of the newer forms of media-based art practice in particular. There was a great start, but the electronic building-site has been left half-abandoned.

These facts cannot be lifted out from the broader context of policy decisions which reflect the ABC's current inadequate level of funding. These broader issues cover the gamut, from penny-pinching approaches to commissioning to the composition of an ABC Board with no significant artist, composer, writer, film maker or intellectual to represent the arts. Even if one agreed with the mainstreaming, 'common-denominator' approach to cultural programs which the organisation has presently adopted, the truth is that the ABC probably does not have sufficient money to position itself effectively, even in the mostly commercial market in which it aspires to compete. In other words, going down-market successfully would require a more substantial investment than the present Coalition Government is prepared to make. One of my opening questions asked whether many in the arts believed that the ABC was any longer a serious player in the field of arts and culture? One quite defensible answer is that it is not and has not been for at least five years, except for a limited commitment to discussion programs on radio and some radio performance work. I realise that some people in more mainstream performing-arts areas and the composed music areas would say longer than five years.

But *should* the ABC be a main player in the arts? It is obvious that with only one channel ABC-TV cannot respond adequately to the mix of both generalist and specialist audiences it is required to cater for. With so little room to move with regard to constructing new audience opportunities or balancing minority and majority tastes, it is perhaps inevitable that one should feel that the range of content options has been narrowed markedly: a single station is required to service all needs—and it cannot do it. Besides, pragmatically speaking, there are already more than enough pressing matters to be addressed. If there is a mainstreaming policy in relation to the arts at today's ABC, then surely this policy needs to be spelt out. Surely, audiences deserve to know how this lateral, inexplicit approach to arts programming will work. In which sorts of programming will the arts be, to use the television term, built in by stealth? Are strategies in place in the organisation which actively influence decision-making and everyday production choices in such a way that the profile of the arts is maintained in these indirect ways? Are news and documentary programs, for example, being given a quota of arts material, a specified number of interviews or features, to fill? A legitimate fear is that, despite all the talk of spreading arts material across the networks, talk will turn out to be not even chat or passing asides. The idea of distributing arts content widely could turn out to be a quiet, unnoticeable—and, indeed, unnoticed—way to forget all about it. Similarly, a plan to distribute composed programs like dramas, acoustic works and music theatre-pieces across ABC Classic-FM, blending them into the mix, could so conveniently turn out to be too difficult, too expensive and too easy to ignore.

If only a few programs and producers are charged with the task of ensuring that material about the arts is made, that the programs get to air, that commissions go to significant and lively practitioners, that new and experimental proposals are invited, that inventive combinations of ideas and skills are put together, that the arguments are waged and won, that new ideas about writing for the medium are argued for, that new ideas about how to represent the arts are ventilated in editorial discussions—for if these matters do *not* constitute an organic part of the editorial and policy process, how can the arts ever flourish? Who will ensure that they do? What is needed here is more than just advice or commentary.[22]

To impact on arts programming an arts forum is required that is much more editorial than an advisory group can be. It needs to work like an arts think-tank contributing directly to broad policy as well as to more specifically focussed editorial projects. Its work as an editorial group should involve initiating ideas across radio, television and online networks and ensuring that integrated planning across and between networks functions effectively. The publicists, the marketing team and the commercialisation team also need to be involved from the outset. After all, how many times in the arts world generally, not just in the ABC, do we hear the complaint that a program, a performance event, is not popular or constructed to attract audiences, only to then learn that a publicist with experience of the market-place had never been invited to the initial planning process? This arts forum of relevant managers and producers could help establish the connections for the involvement of outside arts groups and agencies. It could also monitor how much arts-related and arts-based programming is being made; perhaps it might set down guidelines, take particular programs and their producers to task, if they ignore significant arts news and arts issues. It could even offer the government of the day a legitimate reason for sacking Kerry O'Brien: 'You're under quota! There are not enough arts items on the 7.30 Report!' The establishment of a group of this kind might begin to make some impact. Perhaps, most importantly of all, it would set up a debate, an arts talk, *inside* the ABC.

The unsettled period when the position of Head of TV Arts and Entertainment was a revolving-door may thankfully have come to an end.[23] On radio we may be seeing the signs of some inter-network thinking about how drama, music theatre and experimental feature work can continue to be produced. This potentially good news, however, still sounds far from enough. What has happened with the ABC? Why is there no on-going commitment to well-written, inventively-shot, well-lit dramas, no regular commitment to making well-researched television arts documentaries? Why is there still no sign of a genuine commitment to contemporary Australian music theatre on both Classic-FM and Channel 2? We have been hearing about it for years. Why is there no intensively focussed coverage on arts in both a statewide and a national/international way on all the radio networks? Why is there no week-night half-hour television show for critical, media and public culture debate? Yes, I mean, every week-day night, say, between 9.30pm and 10.00pm. The material, the ideas, the issues of public importance, the theoretical arguments, the chic talk, the gossip—it all abounds out there. Indeed, if we live in the so-called post-modern age, where the art-object, the image and the network of their reception are merging and dissolving into each other, why do we have such unconfident and ineffectual programming in these areas of post-modern culture? Some sort of non-classical, media-savvy approach to art and performance may well be just what that '20-something' and '30-something' audience wants. There are so many more ideas, there is so much more art, than even these brief suggestions can begin to hint at. Why is the audience being hosed down by *Fireflies*?

Ultimately, of course, no media organisation (or theatre group, publishing house, online design company) is going to fulfil all the agendas and expectations which are theoretically conceivable. Nor will its audience. For example, even if more exciting production and arts programming were occurring, would we all slavishly tune in and watch regularly?

In short, if it is true that audience expectations today are complex, structured across different sorts of media, it is also true that the blur between broadcasting and web-casting and electronic publishing—a blending which is at the centre of the cross-media platform—makes any sort of slavishly old-fashioned, real-time attentiveness only one part of media experience. This is the point editor-writer Keith Gallasch has recently made, in discussing the need to tie ABC arts programming in with what he terms the larger 'ecology' of both arts and media practices.[24] Gallasch's ecology includes artists, writers, media groups, theatres, arts initiatives, regional and national arts policies, on the one side, and the broadly defined set of activities which could be called creative research in universities and research-related media companies, museums and galleries, on the other. He envisages what he terms a multi-stranded media model which, like an ecological system, is concerned with preservation, innovation and growth. This model is not driven exclusively by an aim to manufacture audience or compete with commercial competition.

It would be foolish to say that the ABC is not already connecting with these opportunities for co-production, co-funding and collaboration, and in that sense engaging with opportunities in the wider environment. As I write, a co-funding arrangement for the production of four broadband children's movies is announced. There have been many examples, particularly in television. ABC Enterprises plays a very significant role in this multi-stranded approach. The ABC's Regional Production Fund is an open-ended strategy which actively seeks radio program ideas and offers production opportunities. The examples of complex co-production arrangements are somewhat less common in sound, perhaps because the aims and the briefs for radio programs are so particular and also because there is no longer any culture of collaborative investment in composed, edited radio pieces.

Gallasch's concept of a media and an arts ecology engages intelligently and creatively with the future. What, in fact, would happen, if the ABC decided to go it less alone? Is there a way in which a response to the arts environment, a response built on co-deals and collaboration, could become part of the process at a micro level and not simply when the big deals, so to speak, about film series are being negotiated? Again, to say that this sort of collaboration does not operate already would be to overlook some very obvious forms of co-production, e.g. the recording and broadcast of live concerts. The 'Greek Imprints' model also proposes a collaborative, don't-go-it-alone 'ecology' (a Greek word, if ever there was one). This model was based on concurrent communities of interest: in music, in education, literature, festivals, food, in everyday experience, in how we write and represent our lives. Gallasch is probably thinking his way more into the multimedia area, where co-produced, co-written and co-funded work might come from traditionally unlikely media sources: museums, universities, art galleries, media art groups, design companies, art-film companies and artists' studios, as well as from theatre groups and writers.

If nothing else, I would like this essay to provoke debate: not controversy, but a many-sided, evolving debate. Some of the more uncomfortable passages will, I suppose, provoke. But it has to be stated that the ABC's current offerings and its weak policies in relation to the arts are indefensible. It is time, too, that the ABC followed the example of other important arts-related institutions such as the Australia Council, and became more savvy about communicating its ideas and its policies—and the difficult challenges it faces—to the broader community. The arts are themselves a very wide, complex community, in which the ABC traditionally has played a myriad of roles. The days when organisations can fail to articulate their goals and aims, fail to meet with the lobby groups which surround it and fail to be accountable to the general public are long gone.

For one thing, the debate must be renewed regarding a new television station. One ABC channel cannot carry the diversity of material which a globalised, contemporary cultural community like Australia requires. No-one wants to rehearse old arguments, revisit the many old proposals which resoundingly failed to gain federal government support a few years ago, but an obvious suggestion is that this station should be closely interlinked with the ABC's web and online platform. This channel—Art TV— would have an editorial and policy commitment clearly focussed on visual and craft arts, media and media art, film, television features and documentaries, cultural commentary, music, literature, theatre, comedy and performance, both local and international. Would this station be a mainly web-accessed station? Would it be an exclusively ABC-controlled station? Why could it not be run by a consortium of interests, commercial and educational, together with the ABC? Since this station would have no explicit political content, why could it not follow some public radio broadcasters and carry sponsorship and some advertising?

Secondly, the ABC cannot remain the only significant funding source for electronic media which involve the arts and for arts which involve media. A National Art and Media Endowment, independent of the ABC, would be a seeding and development agency, tasked to fund a range of art works and productions which work in the cultural space of arts and electronic media. This endowment would be national, dedicated to television, online, radio and sound-based work. Any production group, television station, community station, gallery, museum, public station or individual could bid for its support. Its budget and its guidelines would preclude its becoming unintentionally an extra funding source for more mainstream, entertainment forms of television, online or sound. The guidelines would need to be carefully formulated not to exclude innovative popular and populist work. The arts funding map would need, with great care, to be redrawn. The fund's criteria, management and selection process would be carefully devised and duplications and overlaps with, say, the role of state and federal film funding taken into account or with existing funding sources at the Australia Council. On the current map, however, there are significant gaps in relation to all sorts of broadcast and online media, mini-series and experimental film, sound work, media artwork strictly defined, to multimedia and traditionally formatted work like art or literature features. Current funding support in this area of broadcast art work, whether from the Australia Council or from the Australian Film Commission, is relatively small. One further impact of such a fund would be to get rid of the assumption that it is only the ABC and a few impoverished community stations which will seriously engage with creative arts. Why should a commercial station not be encouraged to make and broadcast such work? Why do we turn exclusively to the ABC? One reason is: writers, media artists, producers and performers have few other options... but that's another essay!

Both these hastily sketched proposals are highly speculative (see Appendix B). Both address the same perception: that if the ABC is failing the flourishing world of Australian art, writing and theatre, it may be time to look at a more inclusive, more 'ecological' picture of Australian media and their relationship to the more traditional and non-traditional arts. There are several different media environments for the arts to inhabit. It may be time to stop trying to climb over the fence into the ABC's arid backyard—where nowhere near enough is growing.

Some future discussion will need to address those art forms that are themselves directly made from electronic materials: radiophonic work, much acoustic work, but also many aspects of film, photography, performance and design, which are also directly media art. Digital art, the array of art practices which involve digitalisation, the array of media and media art— including a range of film, cinema, sound and electronic arts practices already occurring—are now, and will continue to be, one of the key zones in which Australians make their mark on the world stage. This is inevitable because these media and these techniques, coinciding with our current view of contemporaneity, are the materials of the best current art practices. They are Shakespeare's printing press, they are Whitman's mass circulation book, occurring at a time when the stage, like the book, is as much electronic as real-time. It is vital, then, that there is a place, a creative context and a shaping policy to nurture, encourage and promote these newer forms of dramatic and musical and performing arts. The ABC has a key role here, a most significant role. *My earlier question remains: is not this central creative place the one it ought to be occupying? Isn't this one of its core roles?*

But, the challenge is not only about the new arts or the arts which have re-shaped themselves within the moment of multimedia convergence. Traditional arts—literature, live theatre, painting, dance, for example—do not exist in isolation from electronic media: even their 'real time-ness' and their uniqueness cannot help being defined, or set in relief, by the overwhelming presence of recorded media and broadcast. So the interlinked question of media and the arts is also one to do with a dialogue, with a conversation, between traditional and electronic audiences. It is about the creative and productive interplay between them. More concretely, this creative question concerns, to put it another way, how the Greek radio broadcast threads in and out of the philosophies of now as well as of ancient times, how the poems take on new voices, how the exhibition speaks to the online site, how the live show talks to the radio program. To take another of my examples, it concerns how that creative television viewer watching the new, unbeatable drama series reads from DVD to theatre auditorium to novel and back to the real world. The arts speak to each other and they always speak in the present, in the voices of contemporary media. The ABC has a key creative responsibility here, not the only responsibility, but one which the ABC is well-positioned to fulfil. *Again, is not this guiding, initiating, creative place the one it ought to be in? Isn't this one of its core roles?*

Endnotes

1   Australian Broadcasting Corporation Act 1983, Section 6:c, Australian Government, Attorney-General's Department, <http://scaleplus.law.gov.au/histact/10/5029/0/HA0000100htm>.

2   Liz Jacka, *Arts Programming on ABC Radio, Television and Online* (CPSU, April 2004), available electronically at <www.transforming.cultures.uts.edu.au>. See also Georgina Safe, 'Aunty's Heart No Longer in the Arts', *Australian*, Media and Marketing, 8 April 2004.

3   James Schuyler, *Freely Espousing* (NY: Paris Review Editions, 1969), p. 92.

4   *Essays*, trans. by J.M.Cohen (Harmondsworth: Penguin, 1958), p. 251.

5   *This is the ABC: The Australian Broadcasting Commission, 1932–1983* (Melbourne: Melbourne University Press, 1983). Echoes and analogies with recent events abound in this study of the ABC's first fifty years. See, for example, pp. 322–9, the 1969 Federal Government's attempt to make ABC funding conditional on specified programming decisions.

6   Barry Hill, 'The Mood We Are In: Circa Australia Day 2004', *Overland*, 174 (Autumn 2004), p. 12.

7   Jacka, p. 27.

8   I am conscious of writing this at a time of considerable uncertainty about how and on which networks commissioned drama, acoustic art and the more

experimental forms of music theatre will be broadcast. However, the overall direction of my remarks will, I think, remain accurate: opportunities are decreasing, not only in terms of the amount of new production undertaken, but also in terms of how essential interchange between artists, performers, writers and producers is facilitated. ABC Classic-FM has just advertised a new contract position for an Australian Music curator, a specialist programmer to be employed on a 12-month contract. Perhaps symptomatically, this position seems to be more about programming music already made or already recorded, rather than about stimulating new work, new events or new commissions.

9   John Langer, *Tabloid Television: Popular Journalism and the 'Other News'* (London: Routledge, 1997), p. 43.

10   In fact, the series has received passably good reviews. But I have seen no 'raves'. Nor am I alone in noting how an adjustment was made to its target audience, when the show moved from Sunday to Thursday nights: see Carrie Kablean, 'Fire Worth Stoking', *Weekend Australian*, 17-23 April 2004.

11   Sydney poet Jill Jones and Melbourne poet Michael Farrell have, for instance, both written '*Bill* poems': personal communication from the authors.

12   My list of films is not entirely arbitrary. All have been discussed on the ABC, mainly on radio, though not all have been screened outside the major centres. In short, the balance between how ABC programming repeats or extends expectations, how it creates new expectations and how it fills in gaps is crucial to why viewers turn to the station.

13   Current ABC Director of Television, Sandra Levy, has vocally supported the increase of Australian content on all local television, not just the ABC. See comments

made at the 2003 Screen Producers' Association Conference, and reported in the *Sydney Morning Herald*, 20 November 2003, in reference to the danger that the US-Australia Free Trade Agreement might swamp Australian media with American programs.

14   Clement Greenberg, *The Collected Essays and Criticism: Perceptions and Judgments* (Chicago: University of Chicago Press, 1986), p. 12.

15   Not surprisingly, Amanda Keller's 'secret fetish' turns out to be kitsch and collecting kitsch, according to the Gizmos and Gadgets website. Various prize possessions are listed at <ourhouse.ninemsn.com.au>, for example, a lamp shade 'with a base resembling a traditional indigenous woman', 'a cane-toad coin purse' and 'an Andrew-and-Fergie mug'.

16   Robyn Williams, *Normal Service Won't Be Resumed: The Future of Public Broadcasting* (St Leonards, NSW: Allen & Unwin, 1996), p. 48.

17   Don DeLillo, *The Body Artist* (London: Picador, 2001), p. 38.i

18   *Where Silence Reigns: Selected Prose*, trans. by G. Craig Houston (NY: New Directions, 1978), p. 54.

19   *The Responsibility of Forms*, trans. by Michael Howard (NY: Hill & Wang, 1985), p. 311.

20   The Cat Empire. 'The Chariot' (*The Cat Empire*: Two Shoes & EMI Records, 2003), CD sleeve-notes.

21   While there has been an overall decline in commissioning, it is hard to assess the situation in radio, as various network-based initiatives, in drama, for instance, are yet to be fully articulated.

22   Symptomatic of this problem is the ABC's Arts Advisory Group. 'The *what*?', I hear you cry. You are in good company: very few of the arts administrators, writers, theatre people, publishers and media folk to

whom I have mentioned this group have heard of it either. It only appears on the ABC website, for example, in a three-year-old news item reporting the appointment of its chair. Why, at the very least, you might ask, is the Arts Advisory Board not seeking submissions or running consultations regarding the ABC and arts policy? Why does it not put up a website news item occasionally to let us know what it's thinking?

23   The period 2003–04 has seen three appointments (one in an acting role) to the position. One appointee lasted only a few weeks.

24   Keith Gallasch, 'The Arts Ecologically', *RealTime*, 61 (June-July 2004), p. 4.

Appendix A

Australian Broadcasting Corporation Act 1983

Section 6: Charter of the Corporation

(1)   The functions of the Corporation are:

(a)   to provide within Australia innovative and comprehensive broadcasting services of a high standard as part of the Australian broadcasting system consisting of national, commercial and public sectors and, without limiting the generality of the foregoing, to provide:

(i)   broadcasting programs that contribute to a sense of national identity and inform and entertain, and reflect the cultural diversity of, the Australian community; and

(ii)   broadcasting programs of an educational nature;

(b)   to transmit to countries outside Australia broadcasting programs of news, current affairs, entertainment and cultural enrichment that will:

(i)   encourage awareness of Australia and an international understanding of Australian attitudes on world affairs; and

(ii)   enable Australian citizens living or travelling

outside Australia to obtain information about Australian affairs and Australian attitudes on world affairs; and

(c) to encourage and promote the musical, dramatic and other performing arts in Australia.

(2) In the provision by the Corporation of its broadcasting services within Australia:

(a) the Corporation shall take account of:

(i) the broadcasting services provided by the commercial and public sectors of the Australian broadcasting system;

(ii) the standards from time to time determined by the Australian Broadcasting Authority in respect of broadcasting services;

(iii) the responsibility of the Corporation as the provider of an independent national broadcasting service to provide a balance between broadcasting programs of wide appeal and specialized broadcasting programs;

(iv) the multicultural character of the Australian community; and

(v) in connection with the provision of broadcasting programs of an educational nature—the responsibilities of the States in relation to education; and

(b) the Corporation shall take all such measures, being measures consistent with the obligations of the Corporation under paragraph (a), as, in the opinion of the Board, will be conducive to the full development by the Corporation of suitable broadcasting programs.

(3) The functions of the Corporation under subsection (1)

and the duties imposed on the Corporation under subsection (2) constitute the Charter of the Corporation.

(4)   Nothing in this section shall be taken to impose on the Corporation a duty that is enforceable by proceedings in a court.

Appendix B

Art TV

If it is the case that one of the main problems with the ABC's floundering relationship with the arts is that the Corporation only has one television channel, and is required to deliver on too many different areas of interest, then the following considerations relating to the establishment of a second public channel may be worthy of note:

- Art TV has an editorial and policy commitment focussed on visual and craft arts, music, literature, theatre and performance, media arts, experimental film, arts documentaries, reviews, critical discussion, entertainment, performance, informative, educational, general debate-style programming, both Australian and international.

- Art TV would maximise opportunities to converge its output with multimedia platforms.

- Art TV would keep to a minimum such news and political commentary broadcasts as the station was required to run.

- Art TV could use some sponsorship or advertising as a source of revenue.

- Art TV need not be an exclusively ABC-controlled station.

- Art TV could be funded from levies and lotteries, as

well as taxpayer subventions, in a similar way to the UK's Channel 4.

Most of these characteristics might help protect this station from being dragged down into the government of the day's anti-ABC slur campaign: the station carries little political commentary, it is partly or wholly free of government funding, it is not directly controlled by an ABC Board, which is itself tied to the federal government of the day.

National Art and Media Endowment

If the ABC is no longer positioned to be a key producer of quality drama, music, sound, art documentary and media art, there may be good reason to consider alternative ways of funding such productions. These are some characteristics of the National Art and Media Endowment:

- The fund is dedicated to TV, online, experimental visual, radio and sound-based work.
- Commercial TV, private and community radio, ABC, independent production houses, innovative galleries and museums, theatre companies, individual artists with production track records, art music and fine music recording companies, online artists and publishers could compete for finance and become more involved in the broadcasting of high-quality creative work from writers, performers and artists.
- A broader national strategy acknowledging the connections between public media and creative arts practices would need to be addressed so that the National Endowment could sit within the variety of funding and other arts agencies.
- The endowment's charter and cash to dispense would be such that it was always encouraged to focus on new

and innovative work and not blockbuster projects which could seek alternative resources.

- The endowment would be able to foster collaborative and co-funding arrangements where appropriate and, also as appropriate, offer investment and not only subsidy funds.

Subscribe to **Platform Papers**

Individual recommended retail price: $12.95

Have the papers delivered quarterly to your door:
4 ISSUES FOR $48.00 INCLUDING POSTAGE WITHIN AUSTRALIA

To Currency House Inc.

Please start this subscription from this issue/the next issue.

Name_____

Address_____

_____

State _____ Postcode _____

Email _____

Telephone _____

Please make cheques payable to Currency House Inc.

Or charge: ___ Mastercard ___ Bankcard ___ Visa

Card no. ___ ___ ___ ___   ___ ___ ___ ___

___ ___ ___ ___   ___ ___ ___ ___   Expiry date _____

Signature _____

Fax this form to: Currency House Inc. at 02 9319 3649

Or post to: PO Box 2270, Strawberry Hills NSW 2012 Australia